AF338145

FROM IMPRESSIONISM TO POST-IMPRESSIONISM

ART HISTORY BOOK FOR CHILDREN

Children's Arts, Music & Photography Books

Speedy Publishing LLC
40 E. Main St. #1156
Newark, DE 19711
www.speedypublishing.com

In this book, we're going to talk about the time period of Impressionism to Post-Impressionism. So, let's get right to it!

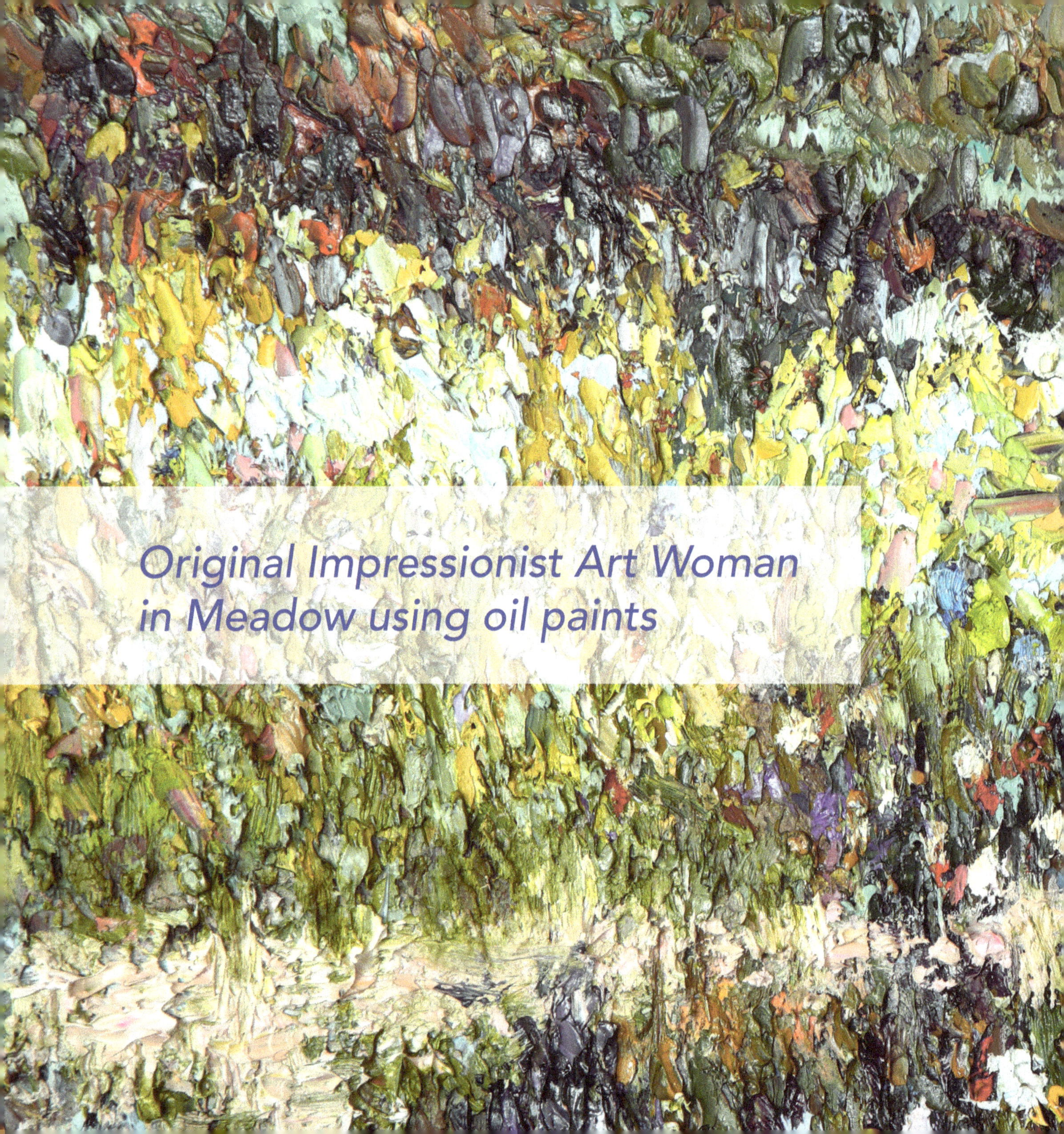
Original Impressionist Art Woman
in Meadow using oil paints

THE HISTORY OF IMPRESSIONISM

Throughout history, new forms of art frequently occur when creative individuals decide that they are tired of doing things the old way and want to try something new. This happened in France in the 1860s. The Salon in France was a group that essentially was the core of the art world.

T
hese art critics had a strong influence on how art was displayed. They also influenced which paintings people would think was **"real art"** and which they would think were crude and unfinished paintings.

The Large Plane Trees (Road Menders at Saint-Rémy) by Vincent Van Gogh.

Then, a new group of young and very creative artists decided to go against the established style of the Salon and launch a completely different kind of painting. These artists wanted their art to show a precise moment of time. They wanted the lighting and the shadows shown exactly as these elements were when the viewer was witnessing the scene.

Painting of circles.

These artists weren't as concerned about the precise details of every person's face or the fine details of every object. Their art represented a completely different style and, to many art critics, it seemed that the style in which their paintings were presented looked completely unfinished.

Boats and pier.

THE FIRST EXHIBIT OF IMPRESSIONIST ART

When the art establishment refused to display their paintings at the Salon, this group of artists eventually decided to do something revolutionary. They would hold their own exhibition! At the Salon, paintings were jammed together on walls, and stacked in tall stacks on top of each other.

Two Dancers by Edgar Degas.

At this first Impressionist exhibition in 1874, the fifty-five revolutionary artists decided that they would display their paintings at the level of people's eyes with plenty of space between them.

At the beginning, these artists didn't call themselves **"Impressionists"** and there's a story of how this name started. The new group of artists included many names that are famous today, such as Renoir, Monet, Degas, and Cézanne. They continued to band together and held eight of these exhibitions in the twelve years that followed.

HOW DID THE NAME "IMPRESSIONIST" GET STARTED?

Monet's beautiful painting, *"Impression Sunrise,"* shows the sun rising above a harbor at the moment of dawn. Painted with blues, greens, and oranges using sketchy, soft brushstrokes, Monet's painting doesn't have any hard lines at all. Instead, the earth and sky are blended together to show exactly what Monet intended, a moment in time where the world is soft and watery around the edges.

Impression, Sunrise, 1872.

The famous art critic, Louis Leroy, made fun of the masterpiece. He said that the painting didn't even constitute an impression. He said it wasn't even as finished as the wallpaper pattern on a house's wall. He meant his comments to be insulting, but the word **_"Impressionist"_** stuck. Within a year,

the word **"Impressionist"** was used for the new style of painting and the movement was on its way. This type of event has happened in the art world many times. What critics or established audiences say is rubbish, many times turns out to be admired and praised a few months or years later.

It took quite some time for art lovers to develop an interest in Impressionism. The movement started in the 1860s and became popular in the twenty years that followed. Today, famous works by the master painters of this period sell for millions of dollars.

The Circus by Georges Seurat.

WHAT ARE THE CHARACTERISTICS OF IMPRESSIONIST ART?

The Academy of Fine Arts in France had been the dominant art school since 1648. They taught their students to paint lessons and display morals through scenes from history, mythology, and the Bible.

Hay Harvest at Éragny, 1901, Camille Pissarro.

The compositions of the former art styles had images that were drawn similar to the ideal images from classical Greek and Roman art. The compositions had hard outlines and were symmetrical. The paint was brushed on very smoothly and there were lots of details.

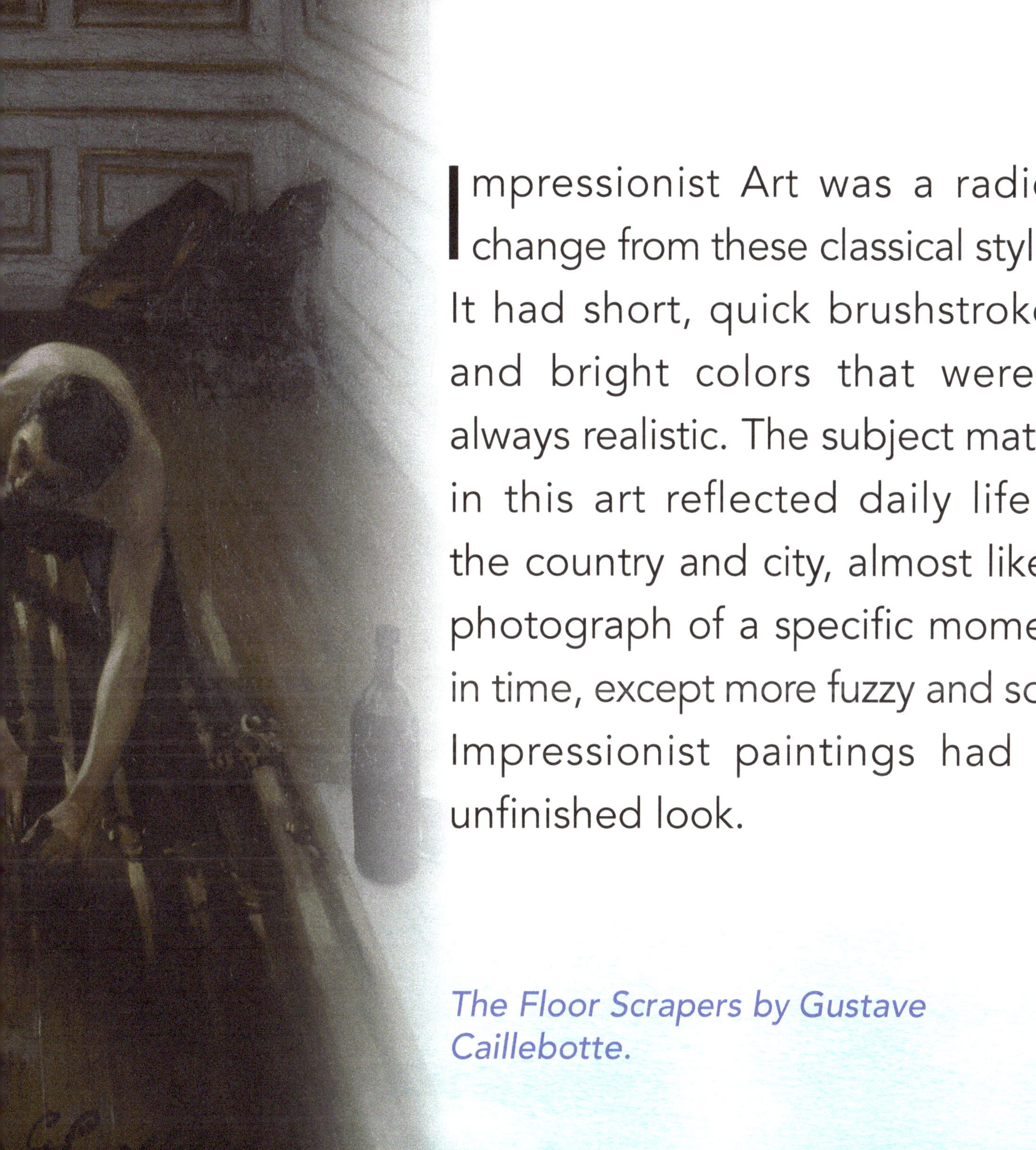

Impressionist Art was a radical change from these classical styles. It had short, quick brushstrokes, and bright colors that weren't always realistic. The subject matter in this art reflected daily life in the country and city, almost like a photograph of a specific moment in time, except more fuzzy and soft. Impressionist paintings had an unfinished look.

The Floor Scrapers by Gustave Caillebotte.

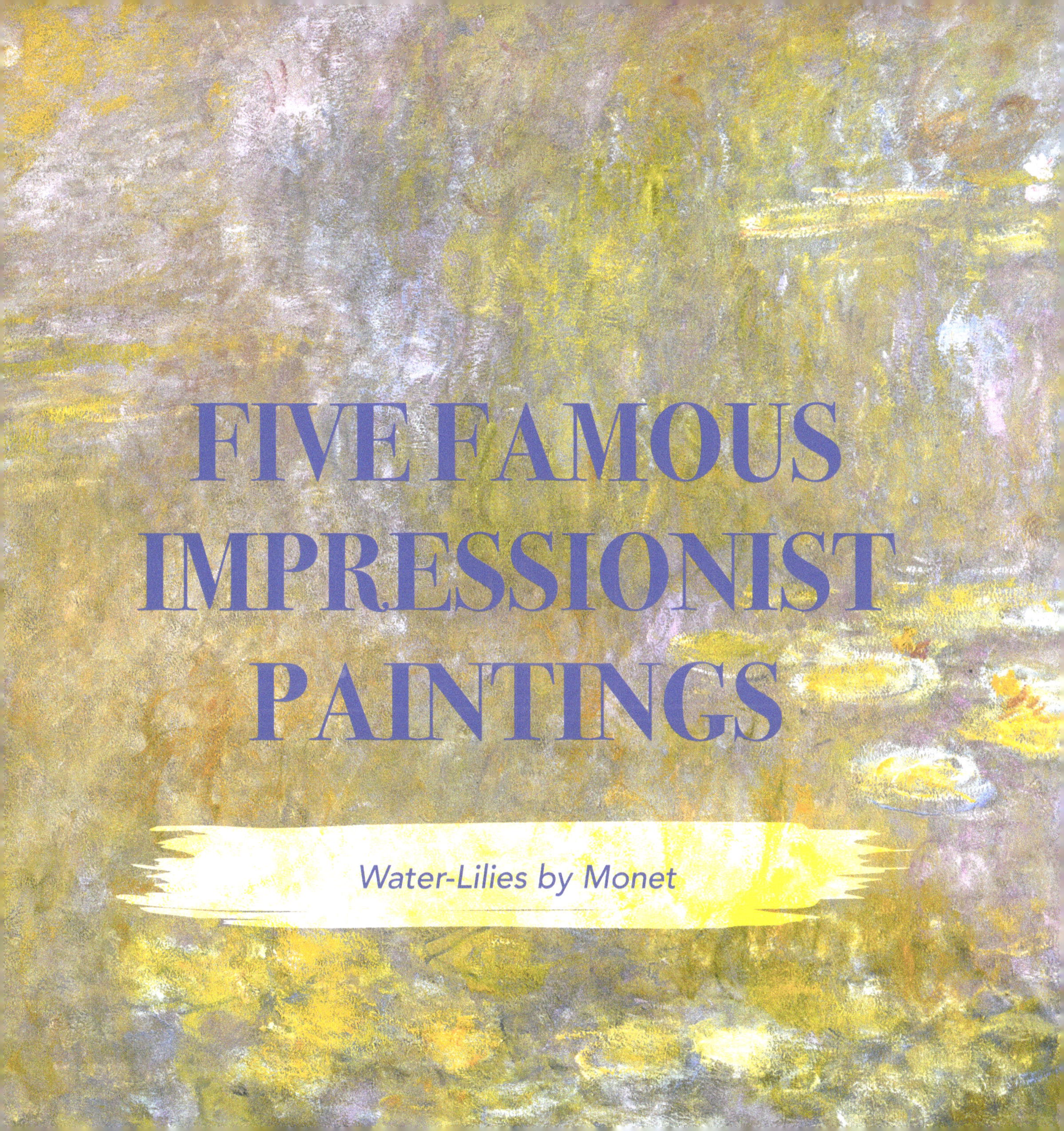

FIVE FAMOUS IMPRESSIONIST PAINTINGS
Water-Lilies by Monet

Water Lilies
by Claude Monet

Monet painted a series of over 200 paintings of water lilies over the course of the last thirty years of his life. Monet actually grew water lilies in his own garden and painted them with complex colors and lighting. The paintings have a serene feeling that fills the viewer with the beauty of nature as the water lilies decorate the water.

The Water-Lily Pond (also known as Japanese Bridge), 1899.

Dance at Le Moulin de la Galette

by Pierre-Auguste Renoir

Painted in 1876, this masterpiece by Renoir shows a happy Sunday afternoon at a dancehall in the open air, which was close to where Renoir lived. People in the foreground are lingering at café tables and the background is filled with couples dancing together in their best Sunday clothes. Light is streaming through the spaces between the leaves of the trees. It's not quite shady and not quite sunlit. It's an amazing combination between a portrait, a still life, and a landscape.

Dance at Le Moulin de la Galette, 1876.

A Bar at the Folies-Bergere

by Edouard Manet

This portrait of a young woman as she waits to serve customers at a champagne bar was painted by Manet in 1882 and was his last major work. The crowd of people in the background is shown in a mirror behind the young woman. The painting provides details about the social classes at that time and gives the viewer insight into the young woman's feelings.

A Bar at the Folies-Bergère, 1882.

Paris Street; Rainy Day
by Gustave Caillebotte

This is Caillebotte's most famous work. The lighting that the painter achieved looks like slick rain on the cobblestones. This painting is more precise than many Impressionist paintings and almost has the feeling of a photograph. However, it captures the light and weather conditions in the precise moment of time, which is characteristic of Impressionism.

Paris Street; Rainy Day, 1877.

Lydia Leaning on Her Arms, in a theatre box
by Mary Cassatt

This beautiful portrait painting shows a young woman waiting in anticipation for the opera to begin. The bright colors show the lighting prior to the beginning of the performance. The sweeping paintbrush strokes give the viewer the feeling that there is electricity in the air.

Lydia Leaning on Her Arms, Seated in a Loge (1879).

WHAT IS POST-IMPRESSIONISM?

Post-Impressionism simply means the period of art that came after Impressionism. This art movement was centered in France as well and came after the work of Manet. The term was coined by a British art critic named Roger Fry. He first used the term **"Post-Impressionism"** and established an exhibit in 1910 to showcase Manet as well as the Post-Impressionist painters. The time period of these painters was from 1885 through 1910.

Two Girls Reading in a Garden by Pierre-Auguste Renoir.

WHAT ARE THE CHARACTERISTICS OF POST-IMPRESSIONIST PAINTING?

This new generation of artists had learned a great deal from the Impressionist painters. They had learned how to use the contrast of light and shadow and how to use experimental forms of color. They added more ideas and stretched the boundaries of art even further with unique perspectives as well as unusual geometric shapes and subjects.

The Cafe Concert, 1878. by Édouard Manet.

FIVE FAMOUS POST-IMPRESSIONIST PAINTINGS
Wheatfield with Crows by Van Gogh.

The Starry Night
by Vincent Van Gogh

Van Gogh's most famous work, this painting shows a scene that he painted from memory in 1889. The sky, which includes the moon, the planet Venus, and several stars, is painted with swirling strokes of blue and yellow. Sadly, Van Gogh suffered from mental illness and did not sell any paintings during his life. His emotional masterpieces are worth millions today.

Vincent van Gogh's Starry Night.

A Sunday on La Grande Jatte
by Georges Seurat

It took two years, from 1884 to 1886, for Seurat to complete this masterful work. He created many sketches to perfect the figures and he used a precise style called **"pointillism"** to complete the painting. This style uses small dots of pure color that are applied carefully in patterns to form an overall image. This serene painting is his most famous work.

A Sunday on La Grande Jatte by Seurat.

The Card Players
by Paul Cezanne

In this painting, two peasants are completely absorbed in the game of cards they are playing. It's a simple scene and yet gives you a feeling of the personalities and emotions of the players. The brushstrokes are bold with thick paint. This painting is considered to be one of Cezanne's best works and one version of this painting was sold for over $250 million dollars.

Card Players by Paul Cezanne.

Sunflowers

by Vincent Van Gogh

Van Gogh created a series of sunflower paintings and they are now some of the most famous works ever painted. One of Van Gogh's sunflower motif paintings sold to a Japanese art collector at auction for $40 million. When this auction took place in 1987 it was the most expensive painting that had ever been sold.

Still Life: Vase with Fourteen Sunflowers by Van Gogh.

Vincent

Curtain, Jug and Fruit
by Paul Cezanne

Cezanne was a master of still-life painting and this celebrated painting inspired Picasso's later style of cubism.

Jug, Curtain and Fruit Bowl by Paul Cezanne.

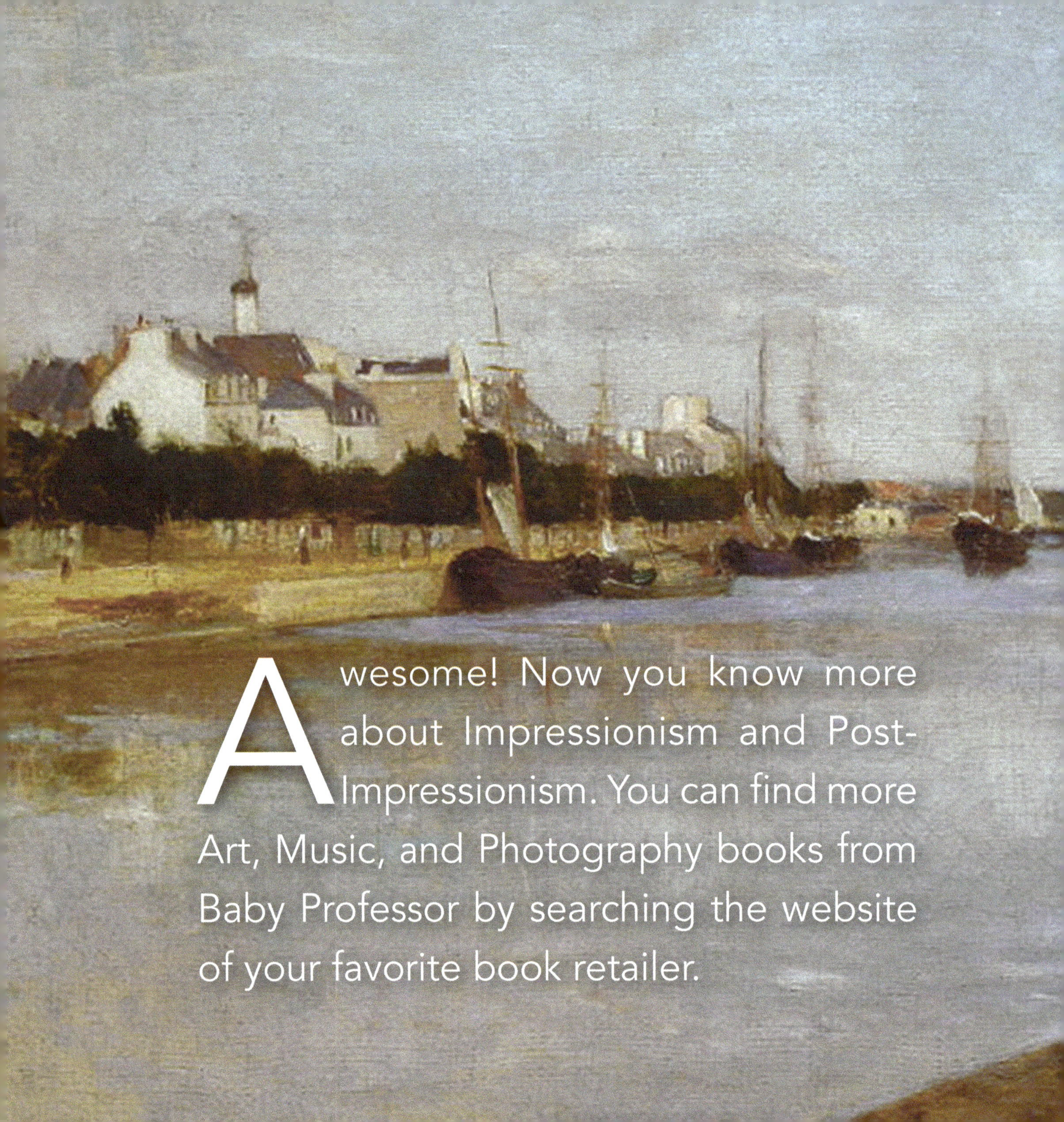

Awesome! Now you know more about Impressionism and Post-Impressionism. You can find more Art, Music, and Photography books from Baby Professor by searching the website of your favorite book retailer.

The Harbor at Lorient by Berthe Morisot.

Visit
BABY PROFESSOR
EDUCATION KIDS
www.BabyProfessorBooks.com
to download Free Baby Professor eBooks
and view our catalog of new and exciting
Children's Books